Table of contents...

Introduction

Happy holidays!! I would have to admit that growing up I had a pretty amazing childhood. As a result of that, I have very fond memories of my siblings and I singing, dancing and just enjoying life. To date, my greatest accomplishment in life has got to be me being the proud, dedicated and loving mother that I have become. My children have become my world and I want for them nothing less than greatness! I want for them to grow up and have amazing memories and feel nothing but warmth and genuine love when they think about their childhood and family just as I do.

Over the years, my family has adopted various traditions during the holidays. Embracing and intertwining these traditions with our culture and our beliefs and adapting them to what is best for, and what best represents our family. Sometimes there are things that we may try one year and never do it again. Then are times that we try something new and we enjoy it and the next year we not only do it again, but we tweak it a little to fit our family. Then the following year or years to come, that "new" thing that we tried and tweaked, has comfortably become ours. Our "fun time with the family", our "that thing that we do"; simply put, our family tradition...

I wanted to put together this book because simply the thought of the amazing times that my family and I have had together absolutely warms my heart and makes me smile. Therefore simply put, I want to share the warmth! As a parent I realize that a child's every development, be it educational, social, even economical, begins within the home. The best way to teach is to do. We as parents should lead by example and there is nothing more gratifying as a parent than to see the good qualities that you have instilled in your child prevail and come to light. My hope is that while building an everlasting bond, together, your family will rediscover what it means to be humble, you will embrace a new faith in humanity, and above all you will remain grateful, not only for worldly possessions, but grateful for one another.

By keeping in mind that not all of these traditions have been adapted by my family, I feel that as the reader you may gain a better perspective and allow yourself to envision what would be an appropriate fit for your family. Even if for nothing more than the experience, try them all. Which ever tradition or traditions that you and your family choose to try, the only rules are to have fun and make them your own!

I am thankful for the opportunity to share this with you and give you a tiny glimpse into the amazing family that I am truly grateful for. I am humbled to have the honor to make a lasting impression of kindness, generosity and unconditional love. My every hope is that you find my words relatable, and that you may find the perfect tradition to be the perfect new addition, allowing your family a unique bonding, learning and growing experience...

Okemah Brianne Holloway

Cookie Giveaway...

Decorate cut-out cookies, package artfully, and give them away...

Sugar cookie recipe..

6 cups of flour

1 tsp baking soda

1/2 tsp salt

1 cup of sour cream (room temperature)

2 1/2 cups of sugar

3 eggs

2 tsp vanilla

2 sticks of butter (room temperature)

Preheat oven to 375 degrees

Mix together ingredients completely...

Separate the batter into two equal parts, roll into balls and cover with plastic wrap. Refrigerate balls for one hour.

Use cookie cutters to cut out cookies into desired shapes...

Lightly dust countertop with flour and roll out dough.

Place 1" apart on cookie sheet lined with parchment paper and bake for approximately 7 minutes. Let cookies cool completely before decorating with buttercream icing and candies you choose. (See buttercream icing recipe) After decorating line a small decorative box with tissue paper. (You can purchase small disposable boxes at your local craft store.) Adorn with a tree ornament, and you have a beautiful and tasty holiday gift for family, friends and neighbors.

Unwrap a story!

Visit one of your local used book stores and purchase 12 holiday themed story books. Wrap each book individually and place under the tree. Each evening of the 12 days before Christmas. Allow the children to pick 1 book to open together. Everyone can gather together by the fireplace while you read aloud from a classic holiday story each day. Not only will the kids enjoy the excitement of unwrapping presents before Christmas, but by visiting and purchasing from a locally owned bookstore you are helping to contribute to an industry that is unfortunately fading away.

Encouraging Words..

Put the name of each family member on a piece of scratch paper, place the folded pieces of paper in a basket and mix them up. Each family member pulls a name and secretly writes an encouraging, inspirational or perhaps even humorous letter to the member who's name they pull...

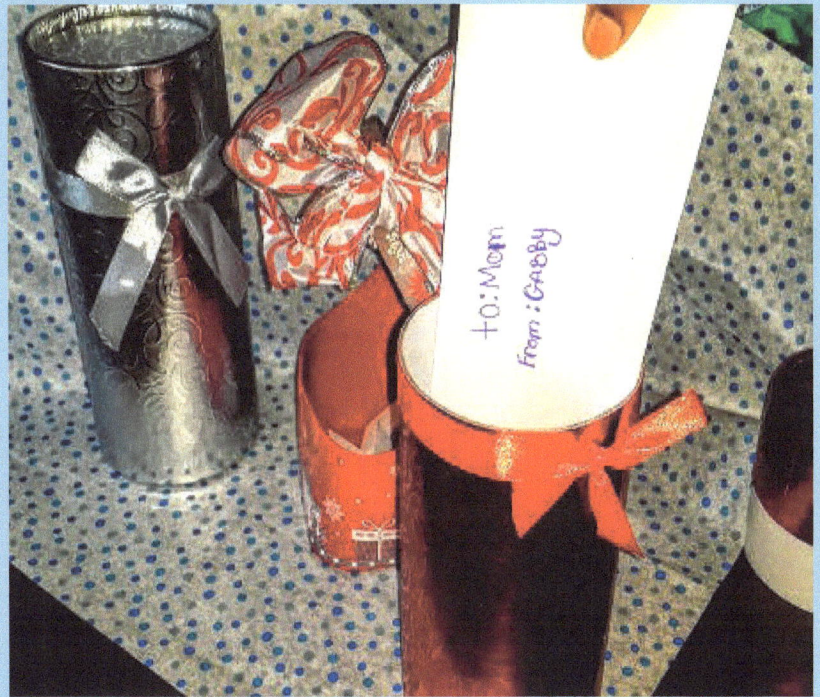

The letters will be sealed and placed into a decorative capsule and tucked away with the holiday decorations. The following year while unpacking and decorating, your family can smile and enjoy the sentiment of the season with heartfelt words of encouragement from one another.

Love Blizzard

Create a beautiful storm of falling snowflakes within your own home!

Using construction paper, use the template to cut out several snowflakes in all sizes and shapes. Be creative, you can use decorative paper or add glitter and gems; anything to give your blizzard a sparkling touch. Place the snowflakes in a basket along with markers and a package of sticky tack. You can place the basket in an easily accessible place near where you want to hang your snowflakes. Each day or whenever anyone gets the urge they can write something that they are grateful for or even an encouraging word on a snowflake and hang it on the wall. You can even attach a snowflake to thread and dangle it from the ceiling. Throughout the holiday season you and your family will have created and inspirational winter wonderland of love!

1) Start with a square or fold a sheet of paper in half...

2) Fold in half diagonally

3) Fold one tip to a third of the way down the opposite side

4) Turn over and fold the next tip to the other side

5) Cut off the top to remove uneven edges...

6) Make random cuts to create your design...

7) Gently unfold to reveal your snowflake...

Learn Something New...

During the course of the year, each family member learns a new instrument, craft or even language! In the holiday season the family will come together and have a showcase and display their new talents and abilities. This not only encourages both children and adults to never stop enriching their minds, but it also enriches and deepens the beautiful bond between family members.

Parlez-vous Français?

Donate

As a family, gather together gently used toys, clothes or household goods to donate to local shelters or organizations that provide for the needy. There are several organizations that will even schedule a pick up at your home for the items! In doing this, your family will appreciate and understand how fortunate they truly are, which is something that we so often take for granted. Embrace the true reason for the season and teach our children to live with a giving heart...

Decorate holiday stockings!!

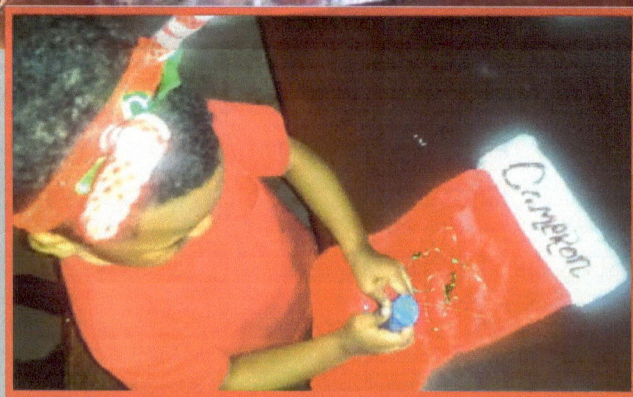

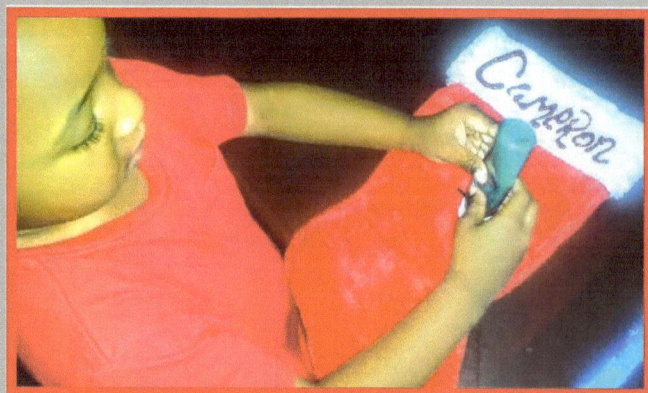

Glitter Glue

Purchase plain holiday stockings from your local craft store. Using glitter glue, decorative buttons and even ornaments, you and your family can enjoy a fun and engaging time together creating the perfect stocking to be stuffed with goodies at Christmas!!

Buttons

Build a gingerbread house!!

Gingerbread Cookie Recipe

3 Cups of flour

1 ¼ teaspoon baking powder

1 Tablespoon baking soda

1 Tablespoon ground ginger

¼ Teaspoon ground clover

1 cup butter (2 sticks)

¾ cup dark brown sugar

1 egg

½ cup molasses

2 ½ teaspoons of vanilla

Preheat oven to 375 Degrees

Fold together dry ingredients

Slowly add egg, molasses and vanilla

Mix together completely

Separate into 4 equal parts

Roll into balls & cover with plastic wrap.

Refrigerate and let chill for an hour.

Lightly dust counter top with flour. Roll out dough and use   stencils to make appropriate cuts. Place 1 inch apart on cookie sheet lined with parchment paper. Bake for approximately 7 minutes. Let the cookies cool completely before the assembling house. Use royal icing (see recipe) to bond the house pieces. Decorate the house after it hardens.

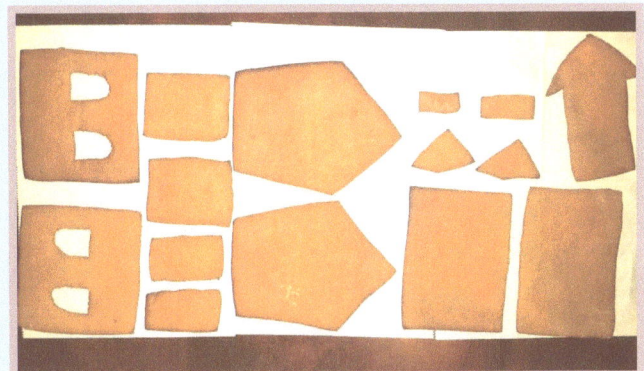

Support our troops!!

Create holiday greeting cards to send to troops abroad ...

Create holiday greeting cards for our Soldiers that may be stationed away from their families during the holiday season.

Be creative, and let them know they are appreciated and how grateful we are for their service.

A small gesture from us may possibly warm someone's heart during this time of the year.

There are several organizations that help to get these cards into the hands of a deserving soldier.

Sing Your Hearts Out!

Make a list of your favorite holiday songs.
Prepare warm cocoa and treats, and go caroling with family and friends...

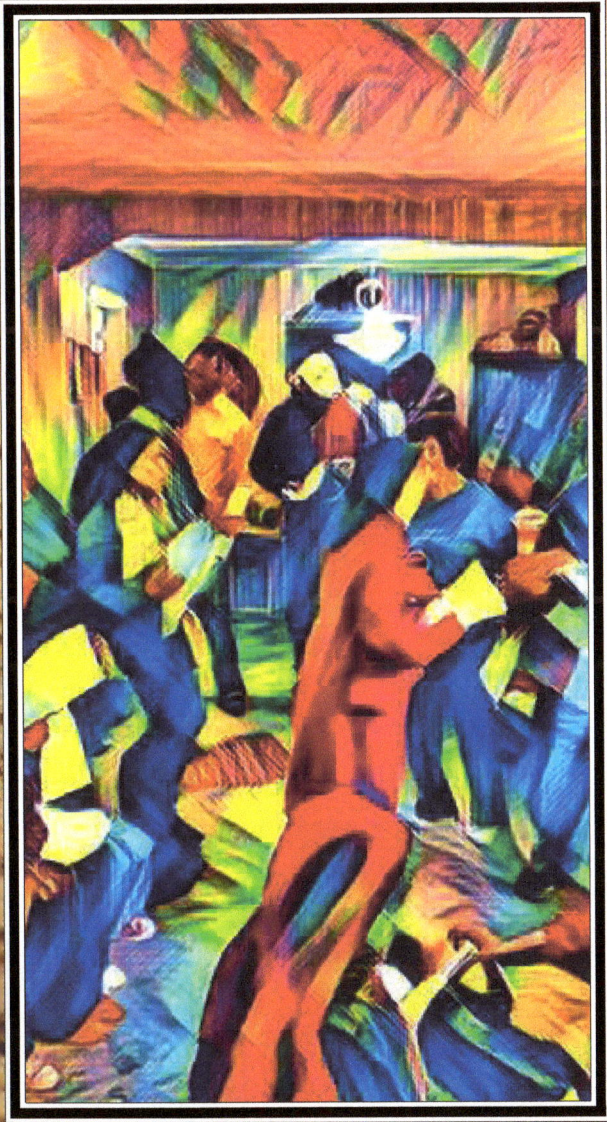

Buttercream Icing Recipe

1/2 cup of Butter (1 stick)
1/2 cup of Vegetable shortening
2 teaspoons of vanilla extract
4 cups confectioner's sugar
3 Tablespoons heavy cream
1 Tablespoon light corn syrup

In a large bowl beat butter, shortening and vanilla until fluffy. Add corn syrup then gradually add sugar and heavy cream alternating between the two an scraping the sides and bottom of the bowl. Recipe yields 2 ½ cups of icing. Keep the bowl covered with a damp cloth until ready for use.

Royal icing recipe (for use in gingerbread house construction)

3 egg whites, beaten

4 cups of confectioners sugar

1/4 teaspoon cream of tarter

In a bowl sift together sugar and cream of tarter. Using
an electric mixer,, beat in the beaten egg whites for about
5 minutes or until the mixture is firm enough to hold its
shape.

Homemade Cocoa

1/2 cup of cocoa powder

1 cup of sugar

1/2 cup of boiling water

3 cups of whole milk

1 cup of heavy cream

1 tsp vanilla bean paste

..Sift together cocoa and sugar, slowly mix into
a pot with the boiling water then gently add remaining ingredients
while stirring. Bring to a simmer, pour and enjoy...

House Roof (Cut 2)

Front Entry (Cut 1)

Template for gingerbread house construction...

Side Wall (Cut 2)

Front Entry Roof

(Cut 2)

Template for gingerbread house construction...

Chimney
Side 1
(Cut 2)

Front & Back Wall

(Cut 2)

Front Side
Wall
(Cut 2)

Template for gingerbread house construction...

Chimney
Side 2
(Cut 1)

Chimney Side 3
(Cut 1)

There are many things that I remember about the holidays; presents, fun and family. No matter how many presents I received at Christmas time, I will always cherish the time I spent with my family. Those memories are precious to me. I hope this book helps you and your family to start a holiday tradition that will last for generations.

Happy Holidays

www.ingramcontent.com/pod-product-compliance
Lightning Source LLC
Chambersburg PA
CBHW042002100426
42813CB00019B/2955